Swan Watch

Also by Budd Schulberg

BUDD SCHULBERG
Swan Watch

PHOTOGRAPHS BY
GERALDINE BROOKS

DELACORTE PRESS / NEW YORK

Calligraphy by Irv Bogen

Designed by Ann Spinelli

Library of Congress Cataloging in Publication Data

Schulberg, Budd.
Swan watch.

1. Swans—Legends and stories. I. Title.
QL795.B57S287   598.4'1   75-5761
ISBN: 0-440-06016-8

PERMISSIONS

Grateful acknowledgment is made for permission to use excerpts from the following works.
"In Common" by Gene Derwood: From THE POEMS OF GENE DERWOOD pub-
lished by October House. Every effort has been made to locate the proprietor
of this work. If the proprietor will communicate with the publisher, formal
arrangements will be made.
"Most she touched me by her muteness" (#760) by Emily Dickinson: From THE
COMPLETE POEMS OF EMILY DICKINSON edited by Thomas H. Johnson by
permission of Little, Brown and Co. Copyright 1929, © 1957 by Mary L. Hamp-
son. Reprinted by permission of the publishers and the Trustees of Amherst
College from Thomas H. Johnson, Editor, THE POEMS OF EMILY DICKIN-
SON, Cambridge, Mass.: The Belknap Press of Harvard University Press, Copy-
right, 1951, 1955 by The President and Fellows of Harvard College.
"The Dream of A Ridiculous Man" by Feodor Dostoevsky: From THE BEST
SHORT STORIES OF DOSTOEVSKY, translated by David Magarshack. Used
by permission of Random House, Inc.
"Jehuda Ben Halevy" by Heinrich Heine: From THE POETRY AND PROSE OF
HEINRICH HEINE, edited by Frederic Ewen, copyright 1948 by Citadel Press,
a division of Lyle Stuart, Inc.
"Leda" by Aldous Huxley: From THE COLLECTED POETRY OF ALDOUS HUX-
LEY edited by Donald Watt. Copyright © 1920 by Aldous Huxley, By permission
of Harper & Row, Publishers, Mrs. Laura Huxley, and Chatto and Windus Ltd.

REFERENCES TO QUOTATIONS

The excerpt from W. B. Yeats introducing the Prologue is from "In Memory of Major Robert Gregory." The excerpts from Heinrich Heine and Emily Dickinson beginning Part I are from "Jehuda Ben Halevy" and "The Complete Poems of Emily Dickinson," respectively. The excerpts from Aldous Huxley and Stephen Spender beginning Part II are from "Leda" and "September Journal," respectively. The excerpted poems from Yeats introducing Part III are from "The Shadowy Waters" and "Nineteen Hundred and Nineteen," respectively. The quotation from Fyodor Dostoyevsky introducing Part III is excerpted from his short story "The Dream of a Ridiculous Man." The excerpt from Nikos Kazantzakis beginning Part IV is taken from his poem "The Odyssey: A Modern Sequel," translation by Kimor Friar. The excerpt from Yeats introducing Part V is from "The Withering of the Boughs." The excerpt from Gene Derwood in Part V is from his poem "In Common."

Acknowledgments

Often a book owes its life to a number of people, who, although they may be unknown to each other, come together as a creative family in support of its author.

To Anne and Ken McCormick, our thanks for encouraging us to make a book of our friendship with Loh and Grin. To Stan Silverman and Sonya O'Sullivan, who gave generously of their time in reading the manuscript and making thoughtful and helpful editorial suggestions. Threefold thanks to Anne Siegel for typing this manuscript through many drafts, and for involving herself in its creation from suggestions of apt poetic quotations to rushing out with bowls of corn when the swans tapped at the window in our absence. And thanks to our neighbors, Fred St. George Smith and Audrey Taylor, who share with us a love of the local wildlife, and were generous with their reminiscences of life on the Aspatuck in the years before we arrived.

We are also grateful to Charles of Charles Photo Lab in North Hollywood for his care and concern in the printing of the majority of photographs used in this book. Special thanks also to Carl Lella for his acts of friendship in artistic assistance.

Finally, Jeanne Bernkopf contributed to this book not only her editorial expertise but an affection and enthusiasm that helped make it for all of us a labor of love.

B.S. & G.B.
Brookside

Be not forgetful to entertain strangers, for thereby some have entertained angels unawares.

—The Bible, Hebrews XIII

Prologue

They were my close companions many a year
A portion of my mind and life, as it were.

—W. B. Yeats

When I was a boy growing up near the Hollywood studio that my father ran, my earliest enthusiasm was not for starlets—those ambitious little animals—or for Model A roadsters with their suggestive rumble seats. No, my childhood passion was for racing pigeons. With my closest friend, who lived on the same block, and whose father helped run the rival film studio, I'd get up at dawn to train our homers. Like racehorses, these winged competitors are born with an instinct that must be cultivated with care.

We'd begin their training by releasing our fledglings one block away. Those who made it back—you always lose a few, supporting the theory that instinct must be reinforced by training—would then be released four blocks away. Then a mile. Soon we were driving twenty-five miles out of what was then a provincial Los Angeles fragrant with orange groves. We marveled at the way our birds circled and circled to find their direction. In a few minutes something seemed to click in their heads, putting them on course. Then, as they sped toward their loft at sixty miles an hour, we'd race them home. An adolescent joy, which I've never outgrown, was to see them loom as distinct specks in the sky and ingeniously single out our loft, come in for a landing, and swoop through the movable entranceway for a well-earned breakfast of cracked corn and fresh water. Even if released as far away as five hundred miles from their loft, it was against their principles, or instincts, to stop for food or drink. A true homing pigeon will starve to death before giving up the homeward flight.

As our racers developed, their range was beyond our ability to drive them up or down the coast fifty to seventy-five miles and get back in time for our first class at L.A. High. Sometimes we would impose them on friends of our parents' who were motoring up to Santa Barbara or south of the border on weekend forays to Tijuana. Would they mind pulling off the road for a moment to release our birds? We'd pick up the empty cages at their homes when they returned. As we grew more professional, entering our best in the formal races of the Southern California Racing Pigeon Association, we would entrust them to a railroad conductor on the old Santa Fe, who—for a modest fee—would release them from the baggage car when the train stopped for passengers in Victorville a hundred miles away.

At first we wondered if it was safe to entrust these precious entries to the hands of strangers. How would we know if they failed to release them? What if the trainmen decided to take Eddie and Peggy and our other stars home for pigeon stew? Hopefully they wouldn't be plump enough to tempt the palate. Pigeons for the table are fattened for that purpose, while homing pigeons are trained down to lithe muscle like prizefighters and racehorses. Still, how could we be sure?

Happily our fears were baseless, and when Eddie and Peggy, our handsome blue-and-white checks, streaked in from their first long flight, we were as proud as the owners of a winning three-year-old Kentucky colt headed for Churchill Downs. We learned how to breed our own thoroughbreds, selecting the superior young males and females and confining them in a mating box. There they would stare at each other through a partition of chicken wire. When we felt that they were ready for the next act of Boy Meets Girl, we removed the partition. Then nature prevailed. It was heartening to watch them live and work together, not merely for that one season but for the rest of their lives.

Years later, prowling the harbor of New York in search of material for *On the Waterfront*, I noticed flocks of racing pigeons circling high above the tenement rooftops and soon learned that pigeon racing was a favorite hobby of longshoremen. Trying to humanize Terry Malloy, the guilt-ridden ex-pug (that Marlon Brando portrayed in the film), I handed on to him my youthful hobby. When he explains to a cynical urchin on a Hoboken rooftop that his pigeons marry for life "just like people," the tough little kid (whose own father had been killed on the docks) says, "Better." The scene wrote itself, with youthful memories of pigeons' fidelity still fresh in my mind.

After finishing a piece of work, a book or a film, I used to reward myself with fishing trips along the Florida Keys or into the Everglades. I felt drawn to Shark River, and Lostman's, moving through a wilderness of sawgrass, cypress swamps, mangrove islands, alligator crawls and rookeries for the most exotic birds left in America. Days when we couldn't raise tarpon or snook were never wasted. For the sight of a flock of white ibis suddenly forming themselves into a feathery cloud floating over the bright green landscape was worth hours of fruitless trolling. So when my brother Stuart and I decided to make a feature film together, we chose this setting to tell the true story of a young Audubon warden—back in the days when ladies didn't consider it decent to appear in public without exotic feathers waving from their hats and gowns. A pure knight of the Audubon, he gave up his life to save the tropical birds from the savage plume-hunters who were destroying one of the great natural aviaries of the world.

One night, when the moon looked like a sun that had forgotten to set, Stuart and I, with our guide Bud Kirk, an Everglades Thoreau, anchored off Duck Rock, an Audubon rookery in the Ten Thousand Islands, offering ourselves as live bait for mosquitoes whose sire must have been Count Dracula. The ordeal was an acceptable price of admission for a sunrise that raised the curtain on a plume-bird spectacular: over a hundred thousand of them—roseate spoonbills, snowy egrets, great blue and white herons, man-of-wars, wood ibis, anhingas—taking off in squadrons mysteriously self-disciplined, silhouetted against a bleeding purple sky.

Later, when I was living in Mexico City, there was always food and water on the terrace wall to attract the miniature turtle doves and *goriolas*, Latin cousins of the purple finch. And when I came back to Hollywood to marry Gerry, whose profession was centered there, we set up bird-feeders to tempt the tastebuds of all the birds in our canyon. One resourceful scrub jay became so tame that he would eat from Gerry's hand. Or rather, he tamed Gerry, for one day when she was outside reading a film script in the hammock, he landed on her shoulder and demanded his lunch. I heard them arguing and came out to eavesdrop. "Cut it out, I have to work on this scene," she was saying. "Use the bird-feeder like everyone else." But noisily (well, how else do jays communicate?) he insisted on personal service. Finally she gave in, climbed out of the hammock, and fed him sunflower seeds from the palm of her hand. Once he had trained her—and then me—Glick, as we called him, would hail us at the top of his voice if we were inside the house, and tap on the window until we came out with his handful of seeds. Sometimes Gerry would call to an empty sky, expertly imitating his voice. If he was within hailing distance, he promptly appeared.

Vacationing in Mazatlán, on the Mexican Pacific,

we struck up a similar friendship with a wild parrot. I always had thought of parrots in cages, or on stands where they perch all day cocking quizzical eyes at passersby who feel compelled to ask them inane questions—"Polly want a cracker?" I knew a caged South American parrot near the great pyramids of Teotihuacán who would tell his inquisitors where to get off, bilingually. And my old pal Bill Spratling, whose statue now stands in the plaza of Taxco, had a tamed parrot on his ranch who would sing *Ay Ay El Rancho Grande* like a drunken mariachi. But a flock of wild parrots soaring overhead in a graceful blur of greens and reds—this I had never seen before. By God, we realized as we watched them circling a stand of coconut palms, parrots aren't feathered W. C. Fieldses—they're birds!

One of them peeled off from the rest and landed on the water-cooler of our hotel's outdoor corridor. He started pecking at the glass bottle and when he began slipping down it, he turned to look at us in frustration. We filled a paper cup and held it out to him. Like Glick, he must have had a human friend before. With cautious steps and watchful eyes he edged closer until, after some moments of careful examination, he began drinking from our cup. After that, whenever we stepped out onto the corridor, he'd leave his comrades perched in the palm trees or flying over them, and land on the railing to visit with us. We called him Buenos Días because that was the only phrase we were able to teach him in the all-too-brief week we were there. In a few days Buenos Días was so tame that he would lower his large vise-like beak gently into our hands for pieces of sweet roll. When it was time to leave Mazatlán we had become so attached to him that we wished we could take him with us. But he belonged there on his tropical shore with his free-flying friends and occasional human acquaintances.

Having to leave them behind is one of the occupational hazards of making friends with birds not confined to cages. There are lots of Glicks and Buenos Díases in this world and they're like people you meet by chance, feel instant kinship with, but somehow never see again. And if you do become involved with them you find that the closer you get, the more you soar with them in their freedom, and suffer with them in their struggle to survive against the elements and the predators.

Part I

Huge, exotic, solemn birds—
Thinkers, too profound to sing...

        —Heinrich Heine

Most she touched me by her muteness—
Most she won me by the way
She presented her small figure—
Plea itself—for charity—

Were a crumb my whole possession—
Were there famine in the land—
Were it my resource from starving—
Could I such a plea withstand—...

        —Emily Dickinson

$\mathcal{A}$ few years ago, after pulling up stakes in California and moving east again, we missed Glick & Co. But when we rented a house near the south shore of Long Island, we began to enjoy the company of mallard ducks and herring gulls. So we decided to take the plunge, buy a house and settle in.

Our seemingly impossible dream was to find a place not far from the city, on the water, and surrounded by woodland. The first place Gerry looked at was on the Aspatuck Inlet (on some maps called River; on others, Creek), a quarter-mile downstream from a County Wildfowl Refuge. After checking out exactly forty-nine other possibilities, she thought it was time for me to see the house on the water at the edge of the woods.

It was a low-lying cottage of weathered shingles,

surrounded by stands of pine, oak and maple, facing an inlet almost fifty yards wide that flows around a heavily wooded, pear-shaped island on its way south to Quantuck Bay.

Instead of following Gerry inside, I walked around the house to look at the water. There, moving slowly just beyond the bank, was a pair of swans. I had seen swans in zoos and parks, at racetracks and other public places, but never before so close, at the edge of a private lawn. I watched them graze along the bank, pulling reeds from the shallows with their bright shrimp-colored beaks. As I ventured a little closer, they both raised their wings as if to warn me away. It was a summer day and their snow-white feathers caught the rays of the sun.

I came back to the house and called in, "Gerry, we have to take it!"

Her smile was full of sunshine. "It's perfect, isn't it! Not too many rooms, this view of the water, and a separate wing for you to work in."

"I'm completely sold."

"You haven't seen it."

"I don't have to. I've seen the swans."

The real-estate lady was pleased. "The swans are beautiful. And they seem to stay around here all the time. The only thing is, I wouldn't get too close to them. They're lovely at a distance, but they really get *mean*."

We told her of our luck with wild birds.

"I wouldn't try it with swans," she said. "I've lived around here for many years. They can be dangerous." And then, perhaps fearing she might be

talking herself out of a sale, she added, "Of course they won't come up on the lawn and attack you. There's nothing to be afraid of—as long as you keep your distance."

As soon as we moved in, dubbing the place "Brookside" in honor of its discoverer, I began feeding the swans from the edge of the lawn, throwing bread out to them as they swam by. Gerry, heeding the lady's warning, urged me to throw the bread from the dock as far out into the water as I could, to keep them from coming close to the bank.

Our neighbors up the river told us the first of the countless horror stories we were to hear: if you encourage swans they become bolder and bolder until they come right up to the house and break the windows with their beaks. That had happened to them, and ever since they had fed the swans only from the nearby bridge that divides our inlet from the Wildfowl Refuge.

Despite all warnings, from neighbors on both sides of the river, I could not resist tossing bread to the swans from our own bank. After a while, whenever they heard the screen door slam they would change course and paddle toward the house. Kneeling at the edge of the lawn, with a handful of bread, I was now only a few yards away from them. That close, I began to notice how different one was from the other. He was much larger than she, with a thicker neck and a black knob, twice the size of hers, at the base of his beak. My guess was that he was at least fifteen pounds heavier, and since he looked double the size of the twenty-pound turkeys I used to raise, I put his

weight at about forty. His large, rubbery, clown-like feet were black while the pen's (for clearly—as we learned from Webster's—she was the *pen* and he the *cob*) were pinkish gray. When they swam together she almost always followed, and when they came toward me at the bank he was bolder and more aggressive. If I made a sudden move toward him, he swelled out his neck and raised his wings, while she backwatered and hissed, sounding very much like a cat.

My efforts to break down their suspicions were not greatly helped by Cricket, the little red kitten we had found on the Refuge road, apparently sideswiped by a car. Carried home, he recovered quickly and was soon stalking the gulls, the ducks and even the swans at the water's edge. Unlike our other cats, traditionalists, Cricket was immediately attracted to water, would walk through the rain when the others ran for cover, and wade chest-deep into the river to hunt minnows and crabs.

The first time the cob saw him at the bank he turned on him, his fierce head and powerful neck pulled back and down into himself, thrusting forward that huge muscle at the base of his neck (or top of his chest). Then extending his six-foot wingspread, raising his head high and aiming it to charge at Cricket, he suddenly ran forward, with a kind of awkward, rolling grace. He charged with all the power of a fighting bull. I expected Cricket to race back toward the house. But our little matador let the force of the charge carry the swan past him, and then turned to tease and invite a second attack. The cob snatched at Cricket's tail, and grabbed at his furry back. Cricket avoided the charge by inches, and then crept back as close as he could, to draw another charge from this unlikely adversary.

So began a strange relationship, a game of cat-and-swan that has continued to this day. Sometimes Cricket will ambush the cob from behind a tree. Sometimes he will roll over and pretend not to notice the charge—much as a matador shows his courage and his control by turning his back and walking away from the bull with insolent grace.

As the swans became daily visitors, we thought we ought to give them names. And, as we were to find out later, we stumbled into the tradition of corny nomenclature that swan-lovers fancy. Because swan couples, with rare exceptions, are monogamous, until death do them part, their guardians are apt to call them Punch and Judy or Sugar and Spice, Kon and Tiki or Eloise and Abelard—that sort of thing. Our inspiration came from the opera *Lohengrin*. After all, Lohengrin was the Swan Knight, son of King Arthur's Sir Percival, who was led by a swan to the rescue of a German princess. My father's middle name, Jehovah help him, was Percival, and my wife was named after a Metropolitan Opera star, Geraldine Farrar. So, we dubbed the cob Loh and the pen Grin because when she snapped at the bread in the air, her beak opened in something very much like a grin. They seemed to take to these silly names good-naturedly, as long as a generous feeding accompanied them.

There is something about swans that has fascinated man from his earliest beginnings. Perhaps it is

their strange combination of sexuality and purity. Their long, expressive necks and their graceful, insinuating movements have made them symbols of sensuality from the dawn of literature and art. At the same time, their feathery white wings and migratory soaring have associated them for thousands of years with the soul and the spirit.

Zeus turned himself into a swan in order to seduce Leda, whose egg produced the fatal beauty of Helen. The swan of Zeus was not exactly an example of fidelity, for Leda was a married lady, wedded to the King of Sparta when the Lord of the Sky had his way with her. But to the ancient Celts (as to the modern Irish), the swan was the symbol of purity. An early chastity test required prospective brides to offer food to the swans; if the swans refused it, the "maidens" were in trouble. In the Court of King Arthur, the wives of the knights were similarly tested, for it was believed that a swan, the soul of innocence, would eat only from the hand of a virtuous wife.

All through medieval legend, and in the nineteenth-century tales of Andersen and the Brothers Grimm, people were changed into swans and back again. There was the tale of eleven princes who were turned into swans by their wicked grandmother. In order to restore them to human form, their sister had to weave each one a sweater (tunic, in the fancier translations)—of nettles!—and remain silent until she had finished her task. She had almost completed that long stretch of piecework when her enemies equated her silence with witchcraft and sentenced her to be burned at the stake. Her eleven swan brothers flew in and swooped down to save her. Still knitting at the stake, she cried out in surprise and joy at sight of them. She had one sleeve yet to finish. That is why only ten of her brothers were able to regain human form completely, while the eleventh was left with one human arm and one swan's wing.

And there were the tales of swan maidens who slipped off their feather robes and hid them after assuming human form. Usually they were then happily betrothed or wed to handsome young princes. But someone would find the feather cape, the taboo or magic seal would be broken, and the maiden would turn back into a swan and fly off into the distance, never to be seen again.

The Irish adore their swans; how beguilingly they tell their fey stories of swan maidens. There was Angus Mac Oc who fell in love with a dream of the most beautiful girl in all Erin. He pursued his dream until he found her by the shore of a lake, with one hundred and fifty other maidens, each wearing a silvery necklace. There the smitten youth discovered that this gathering of maidens was actually a flock of swans. Every other year they assumed human form, but it was only as a swan that the object of his love could ever be won. So the following summer he returned to find one hundred and fifty lovely white swans cruising on the lake, still wearing their silver chains. His dream girl was the most beautiful of all, and when he called to her she came to meet him at the bank. Declaring his love, he changed himself into a swan (in Irish lore as simple a procedure as turning a reversible raincoat inside out) and Angus flew off with his prize to some Celtic heaven set aside for swan maidens and the lovers who sacrifice human form to join them there.

In Ireland a few summers ago I heard so many variations of the interrelationship of swans and humankind that to do justice to them all would fill another sort of book. Their sources go all the way back to the Stone Age and persist on into the twentieth century. In the pub of Groome's Hotel just off O'Connell Street, an actor from the Gate Theater across the way, on his third Paddy's Irish and Harp beer, told me a swan tale from the days of the Trouble. It seems that the celebrated surgeon-poet Oliver St. John Gogarty, in his house on the banks of the Liffey that twists through Dublin, was raided by the Black and Tans searching for his friend Michael Collins, when the rebel leader was the most hunted man in Ireland. Gogarty escaped by leaping into the river. He was a poor swimmer, but a pair of swans came to his rescue and ferried him safely to the opposite bank. In gratitude, he promised to supply the river with a flock of swans, and so, said the actor, they can be found in abundance to this very day, a living, feathery monument to the bond between free Gaels and the white beauties who enjoy dominion on their rivers and their loughs.

When I repeated this recent legend to a local poet in a pub called Neary's close by, he said, "Nonsense, lad. Gogarty was an excellent swimmer, and since he shied away from the striking arm of the movement, the British had no reason to break into his house. And swans have been on the Liffey for centuries."

28

From Gogarty's biographer, Ulick O'Connor, I finally got what seems to be the real story. Gogarty had indeed harbored Collins in the days of the Trouble. But Gogarty dove into the Liffey not then to escape the British but several years later to elude the IRA die-hards who had come to execute him for supporting an Irish Free State that left Northern Ireland in British hands. Gogarty was indeed a powerful swimmer, but the Liffey was an icy torrent that winter night, and Gogarty was drowning. He made a desperate promise to the goddess of the river. If she would spare his life, he would make her a gift of a pair of swans. An overhanging branch came within reach, and he dragged himself to safety.

A few years later, the now Senator Gogarty made good his promise and in the presence of the poet Yeats, President Cosgrave, and other notables of the infant Free State set a pair of swans upon the river, toasting them with champagne and swan poetry. As my actor friend described, they came to be in abundance. And thirty years after, when Gogarty's casket lay on the bank of the lake on his beloved estate in Connemara, one lone swan appeared and swam toward the bier. Was this the swan god, there to transport Gogarty's soul, the legend of Lohengrin come to Connemara?

If I remember my Nordic myths, there was a good deal of hanky-panky between swan ladies and human heroes. Wasn't it Kara who flew over the Swedish knight Helgi to protect him in battle? Alas, brandishing his sword in the heat of combat, he accidentally struck her down. No longer protected by Kara's magic powers, he soon fell in battle, and in turn his death led to the rout of the Swedish army before the Danes. How many talismanic swans the Danes had on their side, legend fails to tell us.

From the time of the Greeks, swans have been soaring into our minds, our dreams, our myths, our poems, our fears and hopes. Socrates dreamed of a newborn swan in his lap that began to sprout wings and then soared into the sky with a musical cry. The following morning he met the youthful Plato for the first time, and knew that the cygnet in his lap had been an omen of this memorable encounter.

According to legend, the souls of good poets pass into swans; so we have Vergil the Mantuan Swan, Homer the Swan of Meander, Shakespeare the Swan of Avon—and, more recently, Dylan Thomas, whom we might call the Swan of Laugharne. Buddha claimed as his the swan that fell wounded at his feet, to teach the hunters that a life belongs to him who saves it rather than to him who takes it. If Wagner, Tschaikowsky, Saint-Saëns, Sibelius and poets down the ages have sung the mystery of swans, it is because the cygnus is the largest, most beautiful, and most provocative to the imagination of all the birds swimming the rivers and flying through the air.

And so, back at Brookside, I persevered in my efforts to improve communications with Loh and Grin. But as they spent more and more time at the edge of our lawn, and as I kept creeping ever closer to them, the warnings from friends and neighbors intensified. The most extreme came from Charles Addams, who lived just around the bend. He arrived in his vintage outboard and his vintage knitted bathing suit to predict the awful things that would befall us if we persisted in encouraging Loh and Grin. His handyman, he told us with a melancholic conviction, had been feeding some swans at his boathouse one day when suddenly they had turned on him and beaten him to death with their wings.

Charley's terrible tale reinforced Gerry's fears. While she still liked watching Loh and Grin through the window or photographing them from a distance, she began having Addamsite visions of their chasing me across the lawn and beating me to death.

But despite Charley and our other neighbors, I couldn't resist trying to break through to them. It was difficult to believe that these serene white creatures could suddenly change into ferocious killer birds. Even Cricket, a tenth their size, seemed to regard them more in fun than in fear.

After throwing bread to them day after day for weeks, I finally reached out from the dock to offer Loh a slice. He looked at me suspiciously with his black beady eyes, then finally snatched at my hand with his beak. I could feel its sandpaper edge creasing my fingers. Loh had not tried to snap at my hand but only to seize the bread.

Behind him, Grin was more cautious. She would not venture close enough to the dock to reach my hand, but she tried to catch the slices in midair as I tossed them to her. On the fifth try she succeeded; and I thought she showed promise of developing into a fair country centerfielder.

At least it was the tentative beginning of a relationship. As I fed them, I would talk to them—"Good swans! That's a boy! Catch it, girl!''—the sort of small talk you make with swans to hold their attention.

By this time I had learned that they were Mute Swans, not the Whistlers or Trumpeters native to this continent but their more silent brothers and sisters, introduced from Europe a century ago. When we got to know them better we discovered that they were not as mute as the word implies. It's just that—like northern New Englanders—they talk only when they have something to say. In the early months of our acquaintanceship it seemed a rudimentary language. But the better we got to know them, the more complexity it revealed.

Hearing that I was determined to hand-feed them, a neighbor of ours, an art designer for a fashion magazine, brought me a pair of knitted gloves as protection against those sharp-edged coral beaks. With these on, one morning in early fall, I placed a slice of bread in Loh's bill for the first time. Both of us seemed to recoil in surprise. Then he grabbed at it fiercely and I was grateful for my glove. After that I handed him another piece, and another, and each time his large black-knobbed beak closed on my fingers along with the bread.

But next day the exchange was a little less frantic. He came to the dock as soon as he saw me and seemed to understand, with the watchful Grin treading water behind him, that I was there only to feed him. And so we began. In a few weeks I was feeding them several loaves of bread a day, an expensive proposition until we found a store where the farmers buy broken, squashed or left-over bread for a nickel a loaf.

Loh and Grin came to depend on it, a loaf in the morning, another in the evening, each slice now offered them from woolen fingers. Within a month, even the skittish Grin was finally stretching her neck forward, daring to take the bread from my gloved hand. But she would hiss loudly as she did so. Day after day she would first hiss and then accept my offering. She could not break entirely the old pattern of hostile self-protection. But each day, while the hissing persisted, she was a little more relaxed with me. She seemed to take her cue from Loh, who was now literally eating out of my hand.

Sometimes our peaceful communion was interrupted, as suddenly Loh would raise his wings, his head pressed back against his chest, assuming his posture of aggression, and I would look around to see that Cricket, the fearless red kitten, had crept up behind me. Or if one of our friends suddenly came down to the edge of the lawn, Loh would again instinctively adopt his threatening posture. But if I was alone with him, he no longer raised his wings or flared out his neck at me.

By Thanksgiving I was able to remove the glove and to feed both of them with my bare hand. Now they no longer waited for me to feed them from the dock. As soon as they saw me come out of the house, they would clamber awkwardly out of the water and up onto the bank, Grin still hanging shyly behind her mate. I would meet them halfway down the lawn, and feed them. At the same time I would talk to them quietly, for my voice did seem to soothe them. But I discovered that Loh had a boiling point of zero. One

morning when the breadbox was empty, I decided to try some toast left over from breakfast. He took it in his beak, discovered it was hard, dropped it in instant anger, puffed out his neck, raised his wings and went for me. I turned coward and ran back into the house. I never dared to palm off dry toast on Loh again. In fact, I found that even bread that was a few days too old would arouse his temper. Of course he was becoming terribly spoiled. But he and Grin were the first pet swans I had ever had, and I'm afraid I wasn't much of a disciplinarian. I wanted them to make themselves at home on our lawn. In time we realized we could salvage dry toast and stale bread by soaking them in water, which seemed to appease both sides.

By the end of the year, no one had been beaten to death, no windows had been broken, and they had definitely enlarged their territorial imperative to include our front lawn. In fact, even the flagstone terrace outside our living room became part of their preserve. Many mornings I would awaken to find that Loh had clambered up the stone steps from the lawn to the terrace and was peering in the glass door, impatient at my tardiness. Grin would wait at the bottom of the steps, not quite confident enough to mount to the terrace herself, but making it quite clear in her own diffident way that breakfast was overdue.

By the time our oaks and maples had shed their leaves, and winter was in the air, we began to know more about the diet of Mute Swans. My sister Sonya, a diligent bird-watcher, had been observing wild swans at her pond on Martha's Vineyard, and insisted that she had seen them dining on minnows and

other minuscule forms of marine life. Discussions on this subject escalated into rather sharp debate, for Gerry and I were convinced that Loh and Grin were strict vegetarians. Either Sonya's swans on Martha's Vineyard were a uniquely piscivorous species, or she had mistaken their objective in thrusting their beaks to the pond bottom. What they were hunting—we felt sure—were not little fish but underwater plants and grasses. All summer the water around our dock had been alive with minnows, and the great blue herons and the snowy egrets, along with a cartoon character identified as a yellow-crowned night heron, would go stilting along the bank to feast on these tiny fish. But Loh and Grin seemed to look on these fish-eaters with pious disdain and went on munching their grasses and algae when not happily consuming our giant loaves of Tastee Bread, vitamin-enriched.

When December cold spread a sheet of ice across the Aspatuck and the swans could no longer break through to the underwater vegetation, we thought it time to feed them something more substantial than sandwich bread. Knowing that ducks and geese are fond of grain, we bought a five-pound sack of cracked corn for Loh and Grin. I handed them a few slices of bread to settle them down and then served them their first bowlful of corn. It was swan heaven! After the first week we were buying ten-pound bags, and then twenty-five. During these banquets they became so used to my presence that I could sit alongside them as they ate. I even ventured to run my hand along Loh's back. Instinctively he raised his wings, but he went on eating. When I tried to take these same liberties

with Grin, she hissed and hurried back to the water. While I am able to come face to face with her when I feed her, and carry on intimate if one-sided conversation, she remains an old-fashioned girl.

One day I walked through the woods to the St. George Smith house that borders ours on the creek. Fred, a fellow Dartmouthman, vintage '15, has lived for more than forty years in what was originally a duck-hunting lodge built by his father, who came to the Aspatuck in the early years of the century and bought the entire inlet as a mallard preserve. Fred's sister, Mrs. Allen, lives behind an immaculate green lawn on the opposite bank. The St. George Smiths know the lore of this waterway from an earlier day when the first commuters horse-and-buggied to Westhampton, a three-day journey.

Fred wasn't sure when the first swans appeared in the bay, but he had heard it was late in the nineteenth century when an early settler introduced a pair of Mutes, whose progeny multiplied until there were swan families in all the surrounding bays. The original pair were known as Charley and Helen and they may have been the great grandparents of Loh and Grin. One day in the mid-40's, Fred found Charley lying on his side, on the dirt causeway between the eastern end of the Aspatuck and the pond now designated as the Wildfowl Refuge. Apparently Charley had been struck by a hit-and-run driver and his right wing was badly broken. He was so helpless that Fred was able to pick him up and carry him home. He and his daughter Audrey took Charley to the vet, who did his best to set the wing and prescribed streptomycin

and aureomycin. Then they entrusted him to the care of Fred's sister across the way. When Mrs. Allen went to fill the prescription at the village drugstore, the druggist asked whom it was for. "For Charley," she said. "Charley who?" said the druggist, "I have to put a name on the bottle." "Charley Swan," said Mrs. Allen.

Mrs. Allen pounded the tablets to powder and mixed them in with Charley's food. Gradually he grew strong enough to waddle down to the bank and paddle slowly up and down along it. But the accident had left him permanently crippled. He would never be able to fly again, or to rise up out of the water and flare his great wings. Meanwhile the traditional fidelity of swans was finding one of its exceptions in Helen. Perhaps she felt that by taking up residence at Mrs. Allen's, Charley had abandoned her. Or maybe it was even more basic. The drive to reproduce is powerful, and now that Charley was grounded he could no longer perform as a true cob should. At any rate the scandal of the inlet was that Helen had taken up with a younger cob who had flown in in search of a mate.

The stronger Charley grew, the more Helen and her new protector seemed to resent him. Together the two of them would attack Charley and drive him back onto Mrs. Allen's lawn. In his frustration he grew increasingly irascible. If his benefactor did not feed him on time he not only tapped on her window, he drove his orange chisel of a beak right through it. With the strength of his neck and his one good wing he even smashed her door. In addition, the feed she set out for him on the lawn was attracting scores of mallards and the lawn she cherished was being—to put it gently—overfertilized. Finally when she was ready to leave on an ocean voyage, she decided that it was time to build a bulkhead to protect her lawn, and to move Charley back to the Refuge, where Fred, Audrey and the other neighbors would throw bread to him. This worked until winter set in. Then poor Charley, whom fate had dealt a losing hand, was found dead, frozen in the ice.

But the tragedy of Charley, Helen and the Other Swan was not yet at an end. Nature seemed to be writing its own version of Hamlet, with the old queen and the new king having to pay for their violence to Charley. Helen and her young consort sailed through the new season, hatching out five healthy cygnets. Then a fifteen-year-old boy crept down to the bank with a .22 and shot the cygnets and Charley II. Helen stayed around for a few more months, seemingly in search of her lost brood. Then one day she disappeared and was never seen again. From such events, we know, the old tales grew, and perhaps there will be a lore of the inlet to rival the medieval fairy tales and the swan visions of the Irish. Meanwhile, the memory of old Charley Swan still lingers on the Aspatuck.

Loh was now a very different swan from the great white menace that had attracted and intimidated us six months earlier. One winter morning when I opened the door to the terrace, he placed an improbable foot on the threshold and was ready to walk right in. I hated to have to close the door in his face, but I was afraid it might rock a happy marriage if Gerry were to see all forty pounds of Loh waddling behind me through the living room and into the kitchen.

Often he would hobble across the snow-covered front lawn and present himself at the picture window, tapping his beak gently but persistently on the pane, not to break it but just to remind us that December was a hungry month for swans.

Gerry was impressed by my progress, but still somewhat worried by it. One morning she went out with a straw basket full of burlap to wrap around her crabapple tree, not realizing that Loh was waiting on the lawn for his free lunch. When she didn't stop to feed him, he went into his stance of aggression, then chased her all the way around one corner of the house. In her flight she dropped her basket, and Loh tore at it, growing even worse tempered when he discovered that burlap is indigestible. Gerry ran into the house through the back door and urged me not to go out. The ghost of Charley Addams' swan-battered handyman definitely hovered over us. But I was convinced that if Gerry had not upset Loh by running away and throwing down her basket, the incipient violence would have been avoided.

It was propitious that just when Gerry's original fear of swans (which we called the Addams Syndrome) had been reinforced by Loh's unmannerly behavior, a book on swans came into our life. It was called *Six Came Flying*—a gift from Anne McCormick, wife of our editor friend Ken McCormick,

43

and bore the improbable by-line of Marquis Mac-Swiney of Mashanglass. Anne had heard us describing our experiences with Loh and Grin and felt that we would find that many of the Marquis' experiences coincided with our own. Of course, his surroundings were a lot grander than ours, a castle on an island in Westphalia. It was there, one day, that six wild swans had come flying in. When MacSwiney had tried to feed one, it had assumed its attacking posture, and he had wheeled in panic and run for cover. But an old farmer familiar with swans taught him how to cope with this problem. You simply hold your ground and raise your arms until you appear to your swan an even more formidable bird than he. Then you crown this performance with an authoritative "No!" The Marquis put this oneupswanship to the test. The cob paused in his charge, studied the giant adversary, then warily turned aside and retreated.

Gerry read and reread the Marquis' description of his triumph before working up the courage to try it herself. Then she went forth with all the hope, faith and sense of adventure of a true swan maiden. Loh was waiting for her suspiciously as she descended from the terrace. When he went into his hostility act, rising up on his feet and spreading his enormous wings, Gerry held her ground, terrified but determined, and spread her arms exactly as MacSwiney had described. Then, calling on all the theatricality acquired in years on stage and before the camera, she delivered a dramatic "No! No!" To her amazement, Loh stopped, studied her for a long moment, and

slowly turned around and started waddling toward the water. Then she followed him and fed him.

So Loh was conquered, or at least on his way to being tamed. After that, Gerry—all five-foot-two and one hundred and eight pounds of her—was like a flyweight fighter, undefeated and on the road to the title. She positively bullied poor Loh. Well, not really. But she did give commands that he obeyed: "Off the lawn, Loh! In the water! I'm going to feed you from the dock." She found that his aggressive posture was largely bluff, and that once she showed that she was not easily intimidated, he backed off. After a while it became a commonplace. I would sit at the desk in my writing room, look out at the lawn and the river, and see a now-confident Geraldine spreading her arms like wings, calling out her imperative "No! No!" and giving Loh a lesson in lawn etiquette for wayward swans.

By the end of winter Gerry was almost as much at ease with Loh and Grin as I had become. She still could not quite bring herself to feed Loh by hand as I liked to do, but she did place bread in the beak of the gentler Grin.

In the first days of spring, when the ice receded from the Aspatuck, we noticed a change in our swans' pattern of behavior. There was a great deal of dipping of heads into the water, at first alternately, and then simultaneously. They would swim close together and circle each other, raise their necks together with their beaks almost touching, in something very much like an old-fashioned film kiss.

As they pirouetted and moved in graceful unison,

we realized that we had front-row seats for their mating dance. Like shameless voyeurs, we watched them perform their rites day after day on the water in front of our lawn.

By the middle of March, with spring coming in like a crazy thing, balmy one day and wintry the next, Loh and Grin began to search for nesting sites on the opposite bank. As far as we could see, Loh would make the initial selection, and Grin would look it over, decide if that was where she wanted to build. They made several false starts, but finally before the end of March they were going at their nest-building intensely. They had settled on a site across the inlet only a few feet in from the bank at high tide, and about thirty feet west of a rickety dock. From our point of view they could not have chosen more opportunely. I had only to look up from my desk to see them building their nest.

There was a clear division of labor, and a close bond of cooperation. Positioning himself nearer the bank, Loh would grab at the bullrush stalks with his beak and then toss this nesting material back over his shoulder to Grin. She would take the reeds and arrange them around her. He also brought back wet globs of floating leaves, reeds and algae. Sometimes, with the field glasses on my desk, I could see her push her chest forward against the front of the nest as if to enlarge it.

The handing back of nesting materials, and shaping them into a nest the size of a bathtub, went on for hours, and then for days. They would pause in their home-building only long enough to swim across for a hurried meal. And then swim back to the nest, he pulling at reeds and beaking them back, she reaching forward to accept and arrange them—in sunshine and rain, around the clock.

Soon we began to notice a change in the feeding pattern. Loh would come alone, eating greedily, but somewhat on edge. Grin would stay on the nest all day, wait for Loh to return and take over; she would then stream across to our lawn, eat hurriedly and turn back to relieve her mate. We guessed that there must be a clutch of eggs in the nest now and that Grin had begun the lonely, hungry month-long task of incubation, with Loh loyally spelling her for brief respites.

When Loh was not feeding or patrolling his territory with chest extended, head pulled back and wings slightly raised, he would take up a protective position about six feet from the nest, swiveling his head, constantly on the lookout for danger. When it was his time to take over, he would circle the nest again and again, they would nod to each other perhaps a dozen times, and then he would come up behind the nest, perch on the rear rim, and the moment she stepped out he would move in and slide his body over the eggs. After we had fed her and she had swum back, the procedure was reversed.

Day after April day, our first sight in the morning was of Grin folded into her high nest. She usually slept with her head tucked back under her wing. Loh would be at his lookout station nearby, but as soon as I appeared on the terrace, he would rise and paddle across as fast as he could. Once in a while, I suppose

when he was especially hungry, he would fly across, his heavy wings making a clop-clop-clopping sound. As he came in for a landing he would lower his large rubbery feet, banking them against the water and skidding perhaps a dozen feet like a seaplane, splashing me if I stood too close. Grace alternates with clumsiness in Loh, performing *Swan Lake* one moment and tripping over his clownish feet the next.

As the end of April neared, Grin spent more and more time without leaving the nest, and when she did appear at the edge of the lawn it was often in the evening. Watching her gliding to us through the moonlight, we could understand why so many poets have tried to capture the exquisite movement of filtered light on the white elegance of swans. Grin would eat hurriedly for two or three minutes but never finish her moonlight supper. As if an alarm were ringing in her lovely feathered head, she would suddenly turn to look back toward her nest, and then paddle back to it as quickly as she could. She was visibly losing weight, her graceful neck beginning to look scrawny as the incubation period went on and on.

Through slashing all-night rains and blustery days she sat there, a motionless white monument to motherhood. Sometimes the tides would rise so high that we were afraid the nest would be flooded and all their labor lost. Again they would work with cooperative patience, to build it higher.

One Sunday morning in May—which a sentimental chronologist had chosen for Mother's Day—we awoke to discover that Loh was acting like a maniac.

To mix our nomenclature, our swan had gone ape. First, with all of his feathers ruffled and his neck pulled back in concentrated fury, he attacked a flock of inoffensive mallards. Then he took off after the gulls. Then some movement a hundred yards downstream attracted his attention and he hurled himself into the air and flew south to Turkey Bridge. Flying back to our dock, he landed with a great splash and began to ride herd on the ducks again. When a small black dog appeared on the opposite bank, nowhere near the nest, he took off after him, driving the terrier back from the bank with a menacing whap of his wings. Then he flew back to the bridge again to take care of some urgent business in that direction. We had seen him fly past our lawn many times, but never in such a wild zigzag pattern as this. Once he spied Cricket on our lawn, and chased him with more speed and desperation than ever before. He even chased me, his old friend.

It was then that we noticed unusual activity on the nest. Instead of settling down low over her clutch, Grin was standing up and moving around, her bill poking around in the nest, as if to adjust the eggs. And then, through the telescope, we saw the miracle of a tiny, fluffy head. Moments later Grin took a part of the large shell in her beak and dropped it into the reeds outside the nest. So that is what Loh's *meshuggener* behavior was all about! He was a revved-up, feathered mess of paternal anxiety: the expectant father, flying crazily up and down the river in search of real or imagined enemies of his family aborning.

Watching the nest through our telescope, we

were able to see the cygnets one by one peck their way out of their shells, until next morning there was a full house—seven! We could not have been more proud if we had fertilized and hatched them ourselves. Seven new little swans, a magical number for the magical bird of Apollo and Lohengrin.

Later that day we were honored with our first visit of the entire Loh 'n' Grin flotilla. Grin led the seven tiny swanlings up to the edge of our lawn, with Loh bringing up the watchful rear guard. He waited about a dozen feet from the bank, on the alert, looking around in all directions. When I handed Grin some bread, she let it fall from her beak, her total concentration on her little brood.

If we had not known they were baby swans, we might have mistaken them for ducklings. For they had no necks! Some were downy gray, others beige, others white, about the size of Gerry's hand, with a small charcoal-colored beak that suggested a pug nose, and ridiculous little wings not even an inch long. Their peeping sounded like baby chicks'. It was difficult to imagine that such tiny, screechy creatures, bobbing uncertainly in the water, one day would be transformed into elegant white swans.

The St. George Smiths were impressed when they saw from their adjoining dock that Loh and Grin had brought their cygnets over to meet us so soon. For swans, they knew, are aggressively protective of their young. A newborn cygnet is vulnerable to every kind of attack. Of course Loh was always standing by to whack an aggressor with his heavy wings. But it was not easy even for protectors as dedicated as Loh and

Grin to keep an eye on all seven at once. So it was a sign of great trust, we were told, that our swans would bring their cygnets across the inlet to the edge of our lawn in their first moments after leaving the nest.

After that visit, they began to come for regular feedings, and soon, like their proud parents, the cygnets trusted us enough to nibble bread from our fingers. Not all of them, only three of the boldest; the others (were they the little pens?) would hold back, like their mama. After a few weeks we became more aware of the differences in their personalities. There was one who was bolder—or friendlier, or greedier— than the others and who would immediately open his small, undeveloped beak to be fed. Another always watched him before trying this hand-feeding on his own. Some had to be talked to and coaxed. And there was one little one who never did accept this personal attention; far more timid than her six brothers and sisters, she always stayed closer to Papa and Mama even when she grew to full size.

During these feeding sessions, even if we tossed bread right under the beaks of Loh and Grin, they ignored it and moved back so the kids could have it. As hungry as they must have been, they never ate when they were in this protective mood. After the cygnets had gobbled the last of the bread, Grin began rocking her body from side to side, working the shallows with rapid shuffling of her webbed feet to loosen bits of underwater grasses and bottom plants that would float to the top. She would nibble at them to show the cygnets how it was done. Their first lesson

in self-sufficiency. Soon in water shallow enough for them to stand, they began to imitate the shuffling motion with their tiny webbed feet. A more advanced lesson, as they grew a little larger, was to up-end and nibble on the underwater grasses near the bank. Through all these early lessons in releasing and gobbling up their own greens, Grin was always the teacher, while Loh took up a protective position behind them, never eating himself but keeping a lookout for predators.

When Loh and Grin decided that the brood had had enough to eat, she turned and headed back for the nest, the cygnets following in a high-pitched chorus, with Loh bringing up the rear to make sure everything was under control. This is one of the moments when a Mute Swan gives voice. Grin would make a low, barking sound, repeating it from side to side over her shoulders as if to say, "All right, children, come along, follow me!" Then all nine would move at identical speed, Grin knowing exactly what pace to set so as not to outdistance them. Their movement was so perfectly coordinated that from afar they looked like a single great white and gray bird moving across the water.

Only after Loh and Grin had them safely back in the nest would one and then the other parent return alone to eat the food they had refused in deference to their young. At these feedings they would eat voraciously, half starved from their weeks of self-deprivation.

For the first several months the cygnets continued to look more like baby ducks than swans-to-be. Only

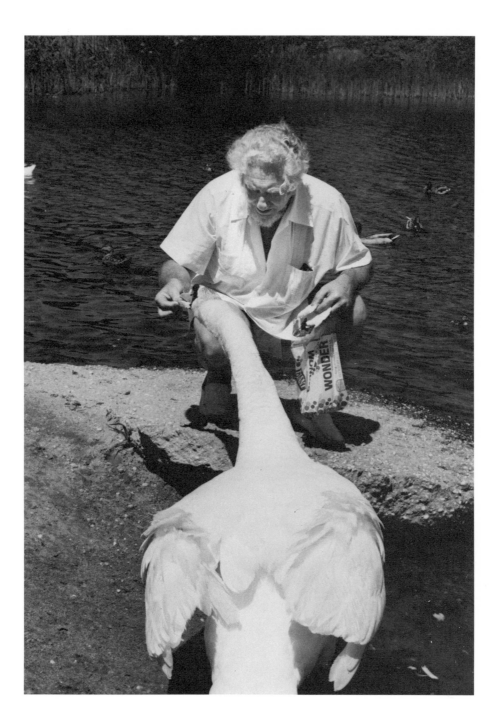

gradually did that unique neck begin to elongate. But they were still in the ugly-duckling stage, with tiny appendages that could not really be called wings, just useless, ludicrous little extremities that did not seem to be growing in proportion to the rest of their bodies. But they were poignantly unaware of this shortcoming. In imitation of Loh and Grin who preened themselves and then rose high out of the water, beating their great wings in a characteristic gesture of swan supremacy, the cygnets would also rise out of the water and wiggle the little downy stumps that they thought of as wings. Six months hence it would be a majestic gesture. Now it was pure Our Gang slapstick.

By the end of summer our seven cygnets were half grown, with long necks but grayish beaks and still-abbreviated wings, definitely full of promise of the swans they were to be, with white feathers beginning to appear among the gray. Even though they were now more than a foot long, bigger than the full-grown mallards, their voices had not changed. It seemed incongruous that these now rather large birds should still be peeping like baby chicks. But their cheeps served a purpose, because if one of them strayed from the group, Loh and Grin would hear and bring it back to the fold. In the early months they had moved in a tight little group, but as they reached adolescence, they had begun to venture first a few feet and then several yards from the flotilla pattern, investigating on their own along the bank.

Again we noticed how much more adventurous some were. The boldest, the first to move away from

his watchful parents, as if eager to see a little more of life on his own, seemed to ask for the name Feisty. Miss Timid still held on to Mama's apron strings; when they were all feeding together, her favorite place was close between her parents.

We had heard of the high attrition of cygnets, that if we started with seven we'd be lucky if two or three grew to maturity. We had also heard of the snapping turtles that would follow the cygnets underwater like miniature submarines, fasten on their vulnerable feet, yank them down to drown and devour them. And of course there was always the danger of the swooping predators; a baby swan can be snatched out of the water with one quick thrust of a hawk's talons. Each time Loh, Grin and family swam toward our dock in their now-familiar formation, I would anxiously call the roll. Once I counted only six cygnets and my heart pounded—but then the laggard pedaled a little faster to catch up with his mates.

Into the fall, the young survived whatever dangers there might have been, until they were almost as large as Loh and Grin. By now they were half white, half gray, and since they had known us from birth, extremely tame. As their beaks grew, a pink tinge pushed its way through the charcoal. It was quite a sight to see them marching across the lawn together to be fed at the terrace when we neglected to meet them with dinner bowls at the edge of the water. Often, I would look from my desk to see Gerry in the hammock reading unconcernedly, surrounded by nine full-grown swans equally unconcerned by her presence.

When we awoke in the early morning, we would see all nine sleeping on the lawn, some on one leg, their heads tucked under their wings. As soon as we came into the living room they would raise their necks, open their eyes and make a swan-line for the terrace. They had become our friends, as boys who used them for targets, or dogs on the hunt, or predatory birds and snapping turtles had become our enemies.

By now our swan family was too large for a dog to attack. And they had grown too big for the turtles to grab by the feet and pull underwater. But the most resourceful of all the predators are little boys. We had heard of a seven-year-old, shortly before our arrival, who had been given a bow-and-arrow for Christmas and was eager to try it on a live target. So he singled out the biggest, whitest and slowest-moving creature in the pond—a grazing pen. The child was delighted to see how well his toy arrow found its mark. It was just long enough to pierce one side of the swan and push out through the other. Unfortunately, there was no Buddha at the Refuge to remind the young hunter that the fallen swan did not belong to him but to the good samaritan who would pick her up and try to save her.

One afternoon, looking up from my desk, I saw a red-headed, freckle-faced boy, about five years old, a pint-sized Huck Finn, tossing bread crumbs to Loh and Grin and the cygnets with his left hand. Which I thought was nice of him until I noticed that in his right hand he held a small, handmade lasso. As he swung the lasso, trying to loop it around the neck of the nearest cygnet, I ran out. "Stop that!" I shouted. "What are you trying to do?" He looked up at me with the gentlest of blue eyes. "I'm just trying to catch me one." And he began to demonstrate a cowboy twirl he must have learned from the previous evening's television horror.

"How would you like it if I took this rope and threw it around your neck and pulled it tight?" I asked him, adopting his tone of sweet reasonableness. He seemed to give my question serious thought. "I wouldn't like it," he decided. "Well then how do you think they feel about it?" I put it to him. He looked at me blankly. Five-year-old Huck Finns suffer from a severe empathy deficiency. He began to regard me with the suspicion and hostility usually reserved for parents and kindergarten teachers. I was about to liberate the lasso from his pink little hand when Loh rose up, now taller than Huck, raised his wings, tilting them forward at their most menacing angle, and began to charge. The lasso artist turned and ran until his red head disappeared through the bullrushes. Then Loh stood on the water and flared his wings in that dramatic display of triumph over vanquished enemies. I knew exactly how he felt. I wanted to flap my own wings at the defeat of that little bundle of treachery.

But our victory was short-lived. A few days later little Red was back for another try. Clearly, it was time for a different tactic. "How would you like to trade?" I asked him. "If you give me the rope I'll give

you this loaf of bread. I feed them because it's fun."

Not entirely convinced, he accepted the exchange. Experimentally he tossed a slice to Loh, who looked up at him guardedly and then began to shake it in the water to break it up. The little boy laughed and tossed him another slice. "This is the way he eats," he said, and he gave a passable imitation of Loh gobbling the bread.

"After a while he'll get to know you and let you feed him by hand."

"I'm not afraid of him," he said as Loh paddled in a little closer.

"And if you feed him like this he won't be afraid of you."

I walked away with the lasso and left him with the bread. Days later, we saw him feeding Loh on his own.

Between Mother's Day and the end of November, surviving autumn storms, tamed and untamed little savages, our neckless cygnets grew into almost graceful, almost full-grown, almost white swans. By early December Loh decided it was time to teach them to fly. Right in front of our snow-covered lawn, he took off with a great clumsy-graceful flapping of wings, flew a demonstrative fifty yards or so, just a few feet above the water, and then swam back to repeat the lesson. Now Feisty was ready to make his first tentative effort to lift off from the surface and follow Papa.

One by one, under Loh's patient tutelage, they were taught to fly. Then came the mighty moment when all nine, the cygnet swans and their proud parents, were airborne. What a sight it was to see them flying in formation up and down river.

For a few weeks more they continued to be a well-knit, happy family. Finally the day came when Loh and Grin decided it was time for their eight-month-old teenagers to leave the security and comfort of home, and to move on to feeding and nesting grounds of their own. We knew that it was essential, inevitable, a part of nature, and yet it was unnerving to watch them suddenly turn on Feisty—that trusting, protected and spunky cygnet—and start to drive him off.

Throughout the summer Loh and Grin had kept him closely at their side, their watchful eyes on him. Now suddenly Mama and Papa were on the attack,

heads pulled back, necks enlarged, wings raised and ruffled. All day the one-sided battle went on, with the confused, strong, but still dependent Feisty scurrying from their pursuit, then trying to circle around to rejoin his brothers and sisters. Finally he sat on the opposite bank, a desolate figure, thoroughly confused. There he huddled, hardly moving, afraid to return to his family and afraid to go out alone into the unknown. On the third morning he was gone, to find his own place in the world. Now Loh and Grin turned their attention to the next victim.

At times we had been tempted to feed the bewildered outcast on the opposite bank, over there in wetland Siberia. But we didn't dare, for to encourage

his return would be to intensify the wrath of Loh and Grin, who had made up their strong and simple minds.

One by one the grown cygnets, some now larger than their parents, were driven off. Since Feisty had gone first, the pair seemed able to tell which was the strongest, the most self-sufficient, the most ready. Whatever their method, they went at it with dedicated detachment, until at last Loh and Grin were alone, together, enjoying their first vacation—as we thought of it—since the beginning of the mating cycle. There were only a few months of leisure before the instinct of reproduction once more became their obsession. As early as mid-January, mating ceremonies began again.

Through the first year I had kept random notes from which the account of this adventure has been reconstructed. And Gerry had taken random photographs. But this time we were determined to keep a diary, at least every few days, and Gerry got a 200-mm lens, so that we could better record our day-to-day education in the mating, nesting, hatching and protective rearing that consumed Loh and Grin each January to December. We felt lucky. How many people had swans living, breeding, growing up and accepting residence on their lawns? We felt a responsibility, amateur Lorenzes, to put down on paper and film everything we could observe about Loh and Grin.

And so we were with them when they entered a world of spring floods, winged flesh-eaters and the idle mischief of inhuman beings.

Part II

Over her the swan shook slowly free
The folded glory of his wings, and made
A white-walled tent of soft and luminous shade.

—Aldous Huxley

. . . the patient faith of waiting. Remembering
that everything is only an episode in the
whole story, and that although one has no
control over the episode, one can gradually
form the whole pattern, however terrible the
setbacks of moments and even of years.

I must put out my hands and grasp the
handfuls of facts. How extraordinary
they are!

—Stephen Spender

Sunday, January 28

On Thursday, the 25th, our swans began their mating ceremony, dipping necks to each other, with a great deal of preening, and finally, consummation, Loh mounting Grin who momentarily disappeared under the water, not far from the edge of our lawn. On Saturday, they began to come to feeding one at a time, and as he did last year, Loh showed more spirit or meanness.

Yesterday they were cruising along the opposite bank searching for nesting sites and this afternoon they were back at the old site, thirty feet down the bank from the dock across the way, Loh beginning to pull up reeds and passing them toward the nest, Grin close by. As I write this, dusk settles over a rainy day and they are back on our lawn munching on breadcrumbs and grass.

Friday, February 2

Cold, snow, drizzling, windy. The river is frozen. Loh used his chest as an ice-breaker to push through to our bank, and Grin followed the canal he made, as they came to be fed this morning. Then they went back to work on the nest. Late in the afternoon, Grin sat on the nest and Loh came for more bread. As it began to grow dark, they performed the mating dance again. One bent a neck to the water and the other followed; arched a neck back and the other followed; cleaned under a wing, the other followed. Soon their actions were simultaneous. Loh swam behind Grin, she put her head down and submerged, and Loh mounted her and held the base of her neck in his beak. Seconds later the mating was over and they raised themselves out of the water, chest to chest, one bill under the other, stretched straight up, facing each other—very nearly as if they stood on the water. Then Loh swam away and Grin did a thorough bathing job. His was more casual.

Saturday, February 3

Complete weather change. Mild and calm. They arrived a few minutes apart—Loh first. She ate greedily —he allowed her to take food that was closer to him in the water—just as she used to defer to the cygnets.

Our houseguest, an ex-fighter who had faced the best boxers in his division, and who still likes to

stay in shape and do roadwork, innocently jogged around to the front of the house and found himself face to face with Loh. Loh doesn't take to strangers and started to attack. Our friend ran back into the house in terror. "I'm not going outside until you get that thing away from me!" he called to us.

I led Loh back to the water, but all day long our friend, who had proved his courage in the ring in scores of battles, peered out the door and refused to venture out until he was sure that Loh and Grin were on the opposite bank. "I'm not afraid of anything with two hands," he was able to laugh now. "I c'n slip a punch and hook off a jab. But how do you fight a swan?"

Wednesday, February 7

This morning there is ice on the ground and lacy snow is falling. Loh and Grin were at the bank early, around 7:30, and I fed them piles of cracked corn, which they devoured. Then they moved off to the middle of the river and resumed their mating ritual.

Now they are about seventy-five yards apart, Grin preening on the little island near the opposite bank, Loh lording it over the middle of the river.

Thursday, February 8

A clear cold morning, with a forecast of snow. Loh and Grin were sleeping on the lawn, heads tucked

beneath their wings. Late risers, waiting for the butler to serve their breakfast. Again they ate greedily of corn served with Brookside elegance on lettuce leaves. Midday we were rewarded with another dramatic mating scene. Pure ballet, a true *Swan Lake*, their wings half raised...Pavlova fans. Then, like the obligatory next scene of a play, Grin went to the opposite bank and clambered onto the nest, moving around to hollow out the reeds. Loh began to act as if on patrol, showing off his power to control the middle of the river and the nesting site. It is all performed according to a harmonious plan that they obey without question. They have involved us in their life.

Monday, February 12—Lincoln's Birthday

These past few days have found Loh arriving—firmly, but not aggressively—ahead of his lady. She follows soon after. Both have their wings aloft. He, by his bearing alone, chases away the ducks who are waiting for a handout on these cold days. Both swans take the bread calmly and allow the seagulls and ducks to eat reasonably close by. He often comes on the lawn or floats slowly while she sleeps on the water. Then they go off together. They seem very close—he is quietly and strongly protective and she is secure and relaxed.

In the late afternoon the river was almost completely frozen, sheets of ice extending from both sides of the bank. Only a narrow channel was still flowing

in midstream, where Loh and Grin were swimming. When they saw us come out of the house, they laboriously forced a canal through the ice to our lawn.

Loh grabbed at the bread and relished the bowl of corn, which he spread messily. Grin was too timid to try the bowl so I threw her more bread. Cricket was there kibitzing as usual, and for comic relief, a pair of mallards arrived, skidding across the ice as they landed. Later I tossed corn into the icy water and Grin inhaled it as it floated, her bill working like the nozzle of a vacuum cleaner.

In the sunset the ice was purple. The swans lingered at the bank, close together, grazing on the cold underwater grasses. Then a blue-black night settled in and they slowly paddled back along the canal they had worked so hard to make.

Tuesday, February 13

Another bitter-cold day with the river frozen except for a channel near the far bank. There Loh and Grin appeared this morning, and when they saw us, he made a tremendous effort to approach, waddling and slipping on the ice until he finally reached our side. He was nervous because Cricket was waiting to play, and Gerry was cracking the ice with a broom since they need the water to swallow the dry bread.

After lunch we found them in the warmer, melted water by crossing at the Refuge, and fed them some muffins. At dusk they forced their way back to

our bank. Now they are pale silhouettes in the blue-purple twilight, their body heat creating small pools in the ice around them.

Thursday, February 15

Soft snow covers the ground, sticks—and still it falls. All the trees and branches are outlined in white. The water flows, however, no ice today, and a crowd of mallards are loitering at the grain dish on the bank. Once again, Loh and Grin performed their mating dance—to our mutual pleasure. The actual mating was longer than usual, and the dance that led up to it more prolonged. He stayed closer to her when she was bathing afterward—but soon, hunger got the better of him and he came for bread and the good cracked corn. After his breakfast, he went to the opposite bank to eat underwater grass and drink a lot of water. She was there, too, and both took the most meticulous bath we ever saw. They looked all downy and fluffed out. He finished and swam to her—she acknowledged him and continued primping.

Saturday, February 24—Sunday, February 25

Over the weekend the river hardened to ice and I watched Loh make that long hard struggle, thrusting his neck and chest forward to reach the bank. Grin held back, but finally used the channel Loh had opened to come to us. But after eating she took a different path over the ice, sliding on her big gray rubbery feet like a clumsy, heavyset lady ice-skater.

Then the weather turned warmer, the river was flowing again, and they swam to the middle of the stream, lovers once more. After the majestic, balletic rising from the water chest to chest, neck to neck, beak to beak, heads raised to the sky, they went over to the site of last year's nest and began to rebuild it.

In these last few days, Loh's behavior has become more erratic and aggressive. He will take a piece of bread, drop it, move toward me for another, and another, virtually attacking me. At one point I stretched my arms out to stop him and he stretched his wings out to counter. Only a sharp "No!" finally stopped him. Meanwhile Grin was arranging the nest or sitting in it as if trying it on for size.

Now he patrols up and down stream with his head high. And he flies more often, frequently out of sight, then suddenly and dramatically flying in to join her, as if he has his eye on her even from afar.

Monday, February 26

When we looked out from our terrace early this morning, Loh was flying downstream toward the bridge. In a few moments he came flying back again. He patrolled in a furious circle, his feathers all abristle, and then hurled himself into the air again, with a tremendous clop-clopping of his heavy wings as he beat his way down toward the bay. Instead of flying low over the water as usual, he rose higher than we

93

had ever seen him fly. It reminded us of his manic behavior the day his cygnets hatched a year ago. But the eggs have yet to be laid in the nest.

Through our field glasses we saw the reason for his wrath. Flying in over the bridge were a second pair of swans. Loh landed in an angry splash in front of our house and wrathfully pushed himself through the water. An old white schooner in the days of the canvas Navy, he charged into battle under full sail. The interlopers saw him, and instead of coming in for a landing, as they had hoped to do, turned back toward Turkey Bridge. Hurling himself into the air again, Loh went after them. They flew on, high over the bridge, and disappeared into the sky stretching to the sea.

Loh followed them over the bridge to make sure that his territorial rights had been maintained. Then he came back, landed on the water in a ten-foot skid, and swam rapidly in a large circle a couple of times. He stood up out of the water, raised his head to the sky and, with an exuberant flapping of his wings, proclaimed his triumph.

Tuesday, February 27

Today, after both Loh and Grin had left the nesting site to graze along the bank, a little boy, about ten, came down the opposite bank with a black dog, and a stick which he began beating on the nest. Gerry called across, with the projective voice of the actress, for him to get away. He heard, answered and ran off. We were afraid Loh and Grin would be frightened but an hour later they were back, once more arranging reeds around the nest.

Wednesday, February 28

A day of rare sunshine, with the gulls circling and the ducks floating so complacently. A late afternoon of spring-like peace on the Aspatuck.

At sunset, through the telescope, we watched what we thought was Grin, working conscientiously on the nest, pushing her breast down and forward to deepen it, and removing twigs and reeds. Meanwhile, Loh swam off to gull island, seeming to admire his reflection in the water. Then she swam over from the nest for a bite of supper, and much to our surprise it was Loh. He was the Mrs. Craig. His chest was stained with mud from enlarging the nest by pushing it out around him. Strange to see a dirty, muddied swan: an elegant Southern planter in white linen who's fallen into a ditch.

As I went down to feed him, Gerry pointed her camera at us, and the moment he saw it he came at her, feathers flared out, ready to strike. Last year I would have been terrified, but now I stretched out my arms to stop him. Grin swam over from the island, I threw corn into the water, which she gratefully inhaled all the way to the bottom while he stood watchfully by, somewhat mollified when Gerry removed the offending camera from his sight. Night has almost fallen and the S-curves of the swan necks are shadowed against the silvery water beyond the lawn.

Thursday, March 1

Clear, bright sun shines on the frozen crust of the inlet. Our swans easily break their pathway through to Brookside. She stays in the water close to the bank, gently and patiently, while he climbs out to demand their breakfast. I haven't time to put down the bowl before Loh grabs at me. He's really crazed these days with his need to be protective. Later Grin comes to join him at the bowl and soon they swim off to mate once more. The more edgy they are with man and bird alike, the more tender they are with each other.

Monday, March 5—Tuesday, March 6

We note the difference in working patterns between Loh and Grin these past few days. Both have worked hard on the building of the nest—he more than she, however. She has begun to take long rest periods—even leaving him to swim and bathe, eat and sleep. He works on.

She seemed about one-third her size yesterday—unusually slim and delicate—and he, on the contrary, half again larger than his normal self. His neck was huge. They ate quite calmly, both separately and together—then swam off to mate again, after an ever more elaborate mating dance.

Today he was in the nest, picking up twigs and dried grasses and passing them overhead, or to his side, building without rest. She was near to him, closer to the water, making a pile of twigs (to be used later? or is it simply instinct?). She swam calmly to be fed and looked so large that I thought it was Loh until I saw her face. After she had eaten for a long time (one full loaf of bread and a bowl of cracked corn), he flew over, his wings making that tremendous clopping sound. He ate calmly, alongside her, as she kept on. We have never seen her eat so much. All day she ate in great quantities, and at many different times. This afternoon, when they both walked onto the lawn to take more corn from the bowl, he stayed close to her, guarding her. Their bodies looked like sculpture—no definition of feathers—this is something we haven't seen before. Another first is that they spent time on land about ten feet from their nest, just sitting and cleaning themselves thoroughly.

Again we remark how much larger she is today. Although the nest seems unguarded from time to time, one has only to watch Loh to see that he is ever watchful. He never just floats—always patrols.

Through Monday, March 12

In spring-like weather, Loh and Grin continue building their nest, spelling each other in all ways:

building, guarding, sleeping on it...They come for separate feedings these days, many times, taking turns crossing back and forth from their bank to ours like white ferryboats. The oil seems definitely lost from the feathers and so they don't look as fluffy as in other days.

Today's mating dance ended with Grin calling out. It sounded like an abrupt, guttural bark. And once, when a young police dog bounded down to the edge of the bank and startled Grin, she let out a low, whimpering moan that sounded unnervingly human.

Two days ago, some young boys crept up on the nest with BB guns and we chased them away. Gentler visitors were a pair of great blue herons who seem to be on friendly terms with the swans and who stood on either side of the nest like bookends. Loh and Grin kept building, ignoring them, and then came together to be fed, leaving the herons with seeming unconcern.

But today it looks as if a new site has been chosen for the nest, about twenty feet away from the other one—and just as dangerously close to the water at high tide. They are starting to build a new nest, all right, but keep coming back to the original one as well. It does make us think that there are not yet any eggs laid.

Monday, March 12

This afternoon they were back on the original nest site. They worked side by side and were finally

so deep in it together we could hardly see their heads. Then they came together to our bank, and as I fed bread to Grin, Loh was very nervous and watchful and finally came out of the water, dropped each bread slice I gave him, and tried to chase me back to the terrace.

Sunday, March 18

A cold, blustery day with snow flurries, raw wind and an exceptionally high tide. The nest, after all that work, seemed to be flooded. But Grin stayed on it, working to rebuild it, while Loh continued to build up the second nest. Instead of working together, they went on with their separate efforts for about an hour.

Then Loh came to our lawn, in a furious mood, so upset that he dropped the bread I handed him, and stepped right into his bowl of corn, tipping it over. Then he went angrily back into the water to chase and bully the ducks, up and down the river, as if he wanted to catch one just to vent his anger. Finally he returned to the first nest, which was now so high that it was a miniature island completely surrounded at flood tide.

Now it was Grin's turn to visit, and we fed her as the snow swirled around us. Loh sat on the high-rise nest, swiveling his head in all directions. Then his beak pointed like a compass. The same boys in blue jackets who had threatened them a few weeks ago were back with their BB guns, aiming at Loh, an irre-

sistible target. I shouted at them, Grin started back, and Gerry phoned the police to come with their sirens and scare them away. Now the boys ran up the hill and around the nest to attack it from the opposite direction, and I shouted louder, "Stay away! Stay away from the swans!" The local gendarmes told Gerry they had already warned the boys. Apparently not strongly enough. So she jumped into the station wagon and raced over to chase them off.

No matter how arduously, even desperately, the swans prepare for their spring duties, it can all be destroyed in a few senseless seconds by kids who feel they have to shoot at something.

Tuesday, March 20

In the late morning two large birds flew in and landed on the edge of the lawn. They had long black necks and I wondered if they might not be a pair of black-necked swans, a kind I had read about but never seen. As it turned out, they were not swans at all but Canada geese.

In flew Loh with a great swoosh. As he landed, our handsome visitors took off, their straight black necks aimed like arrows at the ocean shore. I could hear their honking in the distance as they sped toward a more congenial resting place.

Wednesday, March 21

Loh and Grin have been coming over in tandem, one staying on the nest all day, the other at night. So it is our educated guess that the eggs have now been laid and that we can expect our next clutch of cygnets to hatch in late April. Grin is much more composed, eating calmly but taking only half a dozen slices or a little corn before hurrying back. Loh is still nervous and erratic, sometimes breaking off his meal to start a kind of senseless, obsessive nest-building—like Charlie Chaplin in *Modern Times* when he finishes his factory shift but goes on compulsively performing his fidgety mechanical task. Strange that the excesses of modern mechanization and of age-old reproduction should produce behavior so similar.

Just now Grin swam from the nest site and gently ate half a loaf of bread from my hand. More receptive, calmer, more to business, she visits, eats less than she needs and hurries off, without all the neck-swelling swan-madness of ol' crazy cob Loh. Is this a female virtue, an inner certainty? While he makes a great show of protecting her, she simply goes on about her essential business.

Thursday, March 22

We woke this morning to find, on the third day of spring, half a foot of snow! The cold white world of winter upon us again. All the birds—finches, chicka-

106

dees, red-winged blackbirds, a beautiful pair of cardinals—ravenously at the feeders. And standing in the shallows a few feet from the edge of the island is a great blue heron, his head pulled down into his shoulders against the falling snow. Swimming close to him, a traveling troupe of ducks, lesser scaups, buffleheads and hooded mergansers, playfully disappear beneath the surface and then pop up seconds later like bathtub toys.

And who had left his big webbed-foot prints across the snow—and was now on the terrace looking at me through the glass door? Loh himself. After his long stay on the nest, hunger had brought him right to our door. But he ate only half a dozen slices before growing restless and slightly ornery. Then he hurriedly waddled back on his floppy clown's feet.

Later, it was Grin's turn. She took the bread gently from my hand as I leaned over the water from the bank (in boots, red terry-cloth bathrobe, scarf and black Turkish visored cap—but she doesn't mind). Characteristically now, she acts hungry but really hasn't time to eat. She leaves the fourth slice to the eagerly waiting ducks, and, wings beautifully half raised, turns and heads through the swirling snow to the nesting site.

Now the night is black and the wind is blowing the snow around the trees. I press my face to the window to try to see them on the nest. But it is too dark to see. It doesn't matter. Gerry and I can feel them over there, duty- and nature-bound to protect their nest against this sudden return to winter.

Friday, March 23

Today the snow began to thaw, creating new problems. The tide rose dangerously high, once again threatening the nest. Loh and Grin were in a nervous state, Grin trying to build up the sides of the nest, Loh acting as if he were ready to build a new one *in the water*.

Saturday, March 24

The sun was out and the snow was gone and once again the nest was safely above the water level. As I write this, the sun is setting, and Loh is seated on high, tirelessly reaching out for reeds to build his home ever higher.

Look, he has decided to leave the nest and do some up-ending for reeds on the bottom. I'm tempted to take the canoe over to see if the eggs are there—but I hesitate to incite his protective wrath.

Grin, so lovely in the silver path of twilight, takes only a few pieces of bread tossed to her in the water, and then turns in a smooth straight course toward the darkness of the opposite bank. Loh, silhouetted against the silver-black light, lingers at the bank with Cricket.

Monday, March 26

A gray, quiet day. At 4:00 P.M. I watched them exchanging positions on the nest. Grin spent a few minutes wandering around it, then sat on the rim until Loh stretched and climbed out, and she took his place. I still have to learn the timing of their changing of the guard. Some days they seem to work a regular shift. Often Grin sits from dusk until dawn. Is it safer for her to sit at night while Loh handles the job of patrolling?

Sunday, April 8—Monday, April 9

Grin has answered that question for us. Ever since we returned here from the city Thursday night, she has been planted on her nest, through sunshine and snowstorm, as the spring weather pendulates. From Saturday night to Sunday morning there was a drop of thirty degrees, but through it all Grin sat there stoically. Loh, meanwhile, has been coming to the bank for his handouts, eating morning, noon and night, taking the bread hungrily, and in quite good humor. As far as we can see, Grin has neither eaten nor taken water in days, which explains why a pen loses one-third of her total weight during this long (35-day) nesting period.

Tuesday, April 17

Day after day, and night after night for weeks without food, Grin clings to her nest, motionless most of the time. A visitor looked out yesterday and thought her a huge white stone. When Grin is tucked into herself she does look all of a piece, like good sculpture. Loh, meanwhile, is constantly on our lawn, eating ravenously, as if to make up for his mate's deprivation.

Thursday, April 19

The storms and high tides behind them, Grin sits high on her nest like a queen, while Loh, calmer now, takes bread or munches corn from the bowl on the lawn near the bank. Often he sleeps there. When she isn't dozing on her nest, Grin, ever the fussy housewife, reaches out with her beak and rearranges the reeds around her.

Saturday, April 21

About 2:30 this morning we were startled from sleep by a series of loud blasts from the usually quiet lane that runs to a dead end at the bank of the Aspatuck. "My God, what is that—sounds like gunshots!" I said to Gerry, jumping out of bed and pulling on slacks and sweatshirt. "Help!" she shouted at the top

of her voice, "Help! Help!" And she was out the door, peering across the water to see if Grin was alive on the nest. "Stop shooting! Stop shooting!"

I ran out to the end of the dock. There, in the shadows I could see, or rather hear, a bunch of kids near the bank, honking their horns, flashing lights, partying, laughing loudly, over the sound of explosives that continued to thunder across the water, accompanied by hard rock blaring from half a dozen parked cars. On the other side of the river we could see Grin, just barely, awake now and holding to her nest.

"Cut out the shooting!" I called to the raucous shadows splitting the silence of the inlet.

I was answered with noisy, hostile laughter. Meanwhile lights were coming on in the small houses that usually go to sleep early along this lane. The street was awake now. And so was Loh, who flew over from the opposite bank, incredibly braving the gun blasts to swim fiercely up and down in front of the group that threatened his mate.

"Don't shoot that swan!" I shouted again. This time a spokesman for the hopped-up teenagers shouted back, "We're not shooting! These're only firecrackers!"

"Well, they sound like shots. And it's almost 3 A.M.!" All this time Loh kept patrolling back and forth in front of them, helplessly exposed to bullets if that's what the kids had been using, serving as a shield between them and the nest.

Now a local sheriff was drawn to the scene. What

the kids had been firing, he found out, were cherry bombs detonated in tin cans to make them sound like gunfire. Warned that firecrackers were illegal, as well as dangerous in this wooded area, and that they would all be arrested if they didn't disperse, they called retreat and scratched off in their cars.

We watched them disappear, Gerry, Loh and I. Then he began patrolling his stream again, while the officer cruised the narrow road that approaches it. Once again a precarious peace was restored to the nesting site.

In the first light of morning we slipped raincoats over pajamas and nightgown and went over to see how Grin had survived the ordeal. She was asleep on her nest, with Loh dozing in the second one at its base.

Sunday, April 22

Midmorning there was another disturbance. This time it was two small boys who approached the nest with a handsome, aggressive husky, who had been there several times before on his own, and an Irish setter who was joining in the hunt. Barking excitedly, they came as close to the nest as they dared, the children behind them jumping up and down and shrieking in delight. Loh positioned himself between them and the nest, ready to strike with his outstretched wings, while behind him Grin rose up off the eggs, also with her wings outstretched. The dogs circled around the nest to avoid Loh, but he moved with them, bravely trying to hold them off with his barricade of wings.

We raced over in the car to chase the boys and their dogs away before they could undo all the hard work Loh and Grin had been putting in on that nest the past three months. As we ran down the slope to approach them from the opposite bank, we heard a man shouting, "If you don't take those dogs away I'm going to call the police!" It was a neighbor we had not met before. "My God, they'll kill them!" When he saw us he said, "Swans look frightening but they don't stand a chance when the dogs get to them."

"You see, she's going to have babies soon," Gerry tried to explain to a wind-blown four-year-old with mischievous eyes. "So we must help her protect them. The mother is sitting on her eggs now."

"I know," the little boy said sweetly. "We snitched one already."

"You what!"

"We—put it back," he said quickly.

What with thoughtless tots by day and teenagers out for kicks at night, it's a round-the-clock struggle for Loh and Grin to protect their clutch. No wonder Loh is so high-strung, as they come down the stretch toward hatching day.

Tuesday, April 24

Grin remains motionless on her nest, apparently protected by nature from utter starvation. When we canoed across, her neck looked scrawny and she seemed much smaller. We threw her some bread but she didn't seem interested. At least the weather is balmy now and she can brood there in comfort.

Last year our seven cygnets hatched on Mother's Day. We hardly anticipate this maternal coincidence two years in a row. But we eagerly await the first sight of new life.

It should be any day...

Part III

And all the birds are scattered
—O! O! O!
Farewell! Farewell!

—W. B. Yeats

The Swan has leaped into the desolate heaven:
That image can bring wildness, bring a rage
To end all things, to end
What my laborious life imagined, even
The half-imagined, the half-written page.

—W. B. Yeats

Something was communicated to me
from my silent companion—
mutely but agonizingly—and it
seemed to permeate my whole being.

—Fyodor Dostoyevsky

Saturday, September 1

hy have there been no entries in our swans' journal in more than four months? We lost heart in the diary and put it away.

A few days after the last entry, in the first light of morning, Gerry hurried out to the terrace in her nightgown to look through the telescope trained on the nest. Then she called to me excitedly. "They've hatched! I see five of them! Five little fluffy heads!" I threw on my robe and ran out to join her. Through the strong lens we could see them clearly, their tiny beige-colored heads barely but distinctly visible above the high walls of the bathtub-sized nest that Loh and Grin had kept building higher each time a flood tide threatened to overflow the rim. Five! They had come through that long perilous spring. Every half hour throughout this eventful day we peered through the telescope and field glasses to double-check the census of our new cygnet population.

Next morning we were so eager to see them, we could not sleep beyond sunrise. It was a clear spring morning, cool and promising. First alarm was called by Gerry: "Budd, hurry! I only see *four*."

I didn't hurry. The fifth head would pop up—just as surely as the seventh laggard had paddled to catch up a year ago. But I looked, and looked again and Gerry was right: there *did* seem to be only four little heads in the nest.

We were worried, because we were more sophisticated swan-watchers now than the year before. We had learned some sad facts: More than forty percent of swans' eggs fail to hatch. Of those that do, the mortality rate for the first week is nearly ten percent. And for the second week, over twenty. Almost fifty percent don't make it through their first three months. We had taken our first year's success too much for granted. Innocent and factless, we simply had watched our seven cygnets grow to maturity and fly off to find their own way. The possibility of death, stupid us, had not really been faced, and the actuality of death, happy us, had never occurred.

As we watched, Loh and Grin took their remaining four from the nest, over the bank, into the water.

"What are they doing?...They're too little...the water's so rough!" As soon as they were all afloat, the newborn cygnets were being nudged into the reeds along the bank. Then we saw why.

Suddenly, diving down on them came the great

black-backed gulls. This was the handsome, white-chested, black-winged pair that had swooped into our inlet and onto the grassy island that had been the province of our familiar gulls. They were larger by one-third with heavier beaks curved like hawks'. Our handbook told us that these giant gulls migrated from Canada. On the bird habitat map, there was no indication that they should be here on the south shore of Long Island. But here they were.

Before our eyes they came charging down to attack the newborn cygnets. Tough Loh, so formidable in appearance, could do nothing against these great gulls striking like dive-bombers. The chick-like peeps that had delighted us a year ago were replaced by piercing, high-pitched cries of terror as one by one the newborn cygnets were assaulted, seized, killed.

One little body was floating downstream. The fish crows that had roosted in the branches overhanging the nest were competing now with the great gulls to rip it apart.

Gerry screamed and, crying, picked up stones and flung them at the predators. Like throwing pebbles at San Clemente.

Christ Jesus, I mourned, is nothing not a war, is nothing simple fun and joy and life?

Of the five cygnets, only one was left. Keeping him close between them for protection, Loh and Grin swam south with him. So tiny he was, trying to keep up with them, a baby refugee. There was a strong wind roughing up the water and it seemed as if the lone survivor could not keep his head above the waves. They were followed by the great black-backed bastards (now their official name at Brookside) and the B-B-B's were followed in turn by their legion of crows who were cawing, laughing—the sound is terrible: a dirty, nasty Hah-hah-hah!—the hyena laugh of picking up the pieces, the little pieces of the swans that were to be.

On this mean, windy day, with the river roiling, we waited and watched. An hour later Loh and Grin swam slowly back toward us, alone. It was over. All those months, all that work. All that courage—which nonsentimentalists may simply call *instinct*. All that whateveritis. We were in no mood for zoological discussion. All we knew is that we had lost the five little cygnets, and we didn't want to hear about Darwin and the survival of the fittest, or even the balance, so precarious, of nature.

We tried to beckon Loh and Grin with bread, but they were bereft. Or perhaps, preoccupied. As we watched from our lawn, helpless, they returned to their ravished nest. Overhead, the trees were full of crows caw-cawing, haw-hawing. Cruel laughter.

Trying to stay as far away as possible from this rustic version of a street gang on the prowl, a mallard mother whose struggle to protect her eight newborn ducklings had been going on for several days, led them hurriedly upstream toward the Refuge. They huddled so closely around her for protection that they looked like tiny appendages of the mother bird. But to no avail. The first time a wave separated one of the ducklings from the group, a great black-backed gull swooped down for a tasty dessert, seizing it in his beak and flying off. A few seconds later we were screaming at the gull's mate who followed him down to pick off another. The frantic mallard hen tried to hide her defenseless brood in the rushes that fringe the creek. We shouted, banged pots together and threw stones at the gulls to frighten them off. But in a few minutes only three of the eight ducklings were still alive.

Stunned by this latest assault, Gerry and I just stood there, drained by a rage that could find no outlet. Now, on the opposite bank, we watched Loh and Grin in the aftermath of their loss.

"Look, Budd, they've gone back to the nest. They're looking for the babies."

"Christ, I can't stand it. They're poking into the reeds where they tried to hide them."

"They're swimming back to the nest again, with all those crows on it!"

"Now they're going back toward the bridge. Where they lost the last one."

"My God, they're starting to build another nest!"

And so they were, instinctively, compulsively, only a few feet from the now-desolate one that had been their home for the past four months. But the nest-building was confused and erratic. They would work at it industriously for half an hour, and then move on to another section of the opposite bank and frantically loosen reeds and arrange them in a circle around them again. And all through this ordeal, the trees above and around them were alive with crows who kept on caw-caw-cawing. The carnage had attracted hundreds of them. Last year we had seen only a handful. The sound that assaulted us as dirty, challenging laughter was unnerving counterpoint to Loh and Grin's silent, futile, driven effort to restore what they had lost.

For another week of desperation, Loh and Grin pressed on with their compulsive nest-building, up and down the opposite bank. Occasionally they would return to our lawn, but they were too distracted to eat. The great gulls looked on.

And then, one morning, Loh and Grin were gone. We drove around, over the Turkey Bridge into Westhampton, then to the Refuge road, and finally over the Quogue Bridge across Quantuck Bay, searching for them.

A week or so later I spotted Loh, in the Wildfowl Refuge near the mouth of the Aspatuck, on the north side of Brook Road. He heard me call, came over and took some bread from my hand. I did not see Grin. A few weeks later, after I had begun dropping by to visit with Loh, I discovered Grin, half hidden in the reeds far back in the pond. I called to her but she would not come.

Then, in midsummer, they disappeared entirely. Our lawn and river front looked deserted without them. Cricket missed them too. He spent less time at the edge of the lawn now. Occasionally from the dock I would still call, "Here, Loh . . . Here, Grin!" and Cricket would come running up to wait with me. But their elegant white presence never materialized. We had stopped keeping the diary on the day of the massacre—our own Long Island My Lai, the slaughter of the innocents. And now that Loh and Grin were gone, we put our notebook away. There was nothing more to record.

Part IV

. . . There's much on earth I've suffered,
*   yet I don't repent,*
And now that life's come back,
I'll take the same road twice!

—Nikos Kazantzakis

*O*ur swanless summer passed. Gerry flew off to the Coast for a TV series. In September I went out to visit with her in the Hollywood that had been the bucolic home of my childhood when the air was clear and you *could* see Catalina from the sun-browned hills overlooking Sunset Boulevard.

Then I drove on to Mexico City, to another world that holds a kind of nostalgia for me. It was there that a telephone call came from our secretary, Annie, who, as she likes to put it, was also "into birds." All the way from the Aspatuck to our flat in the heart of the city of Mexico, she sang out the news, "They're back! Your swans. They've come home."

It was time to put an end to wandering and get to work. The day I returned, Brookside was golden in the October sun. They had been gone five months.

Would they still remember us? How much do swans remember?

When I didn't see them, I hurried out to the end of the dock and called out, "Here, Loh! Here, Grin!" In a few moments they came flying toward me, greeting me at the bank, Loh taking the bread from my hand even more gently than before. And Grin, more nervously, back-pedaling her rubbery gray feet,

stretching her elegant neck forward to snatch the bread with her bright coral beak.

That evening Gerry also flew in, and the following morning it was reassuring to look out from our bedroom window and see them in the soft glow of early light, sleeping on their lawn, heads tucked under their wings, Cricket sleeping close by. Waiting for breakfast once again.

Through the rest of October and on into January, they were gentle and friendly, and once more I was able to reach out and stroke Loh's back as he took the bread from my hand and sometimes waddled back to the bank to soften it in the water before swallowing.

Behind them, hundreds of herring gulls have gathered, and among them, a pair of the great blackbacks that devoured their newborn cygnets last spring.

But Loh and Grin seem to have forgotten. They float or glide past their old enemies as if the massacre had never occurred. We felt an impulse to call out to

them, to alert them to the danger that lurks on our inlet come the next hatching season.

Loh and Grin had a projective memory sufficiently receptive to permit them to return to us after an absence of many months, to respond to our calls and to take the bread from our hands with obvious solicitude for our fingers. So, if they remember us who befriend them, why do they fail, in the off-season, to remember their enemies? Is it because what we are doing for them we are doing at that moment, while the threat from the black-backs lies in some unimagined future? Perhaps our swans could give existentialist lessons to Sartre.

Now it is mid-February, the river is frozen solid once again and a foot of snow covers the ground. From my desk facing the Aspatuck, I see our swans fly past, improbable white missiles, their long necks thrust forward, their great wings almost brushing the ice.

Monday, February 18

The river is still frozen, but with a few soft spots, and
Loh and Grin skidded their way across the ice to us.
Grin followed as always…
    Suddenly she stopped walking and sat down.

When Loh reached the bank, I stepped out onto the ice, handed him a piece of sprouted rye, and slid a few slices over to Grin. She didn't move forward to get them. She tried, but we realized she was stuck in the ice. We had heard of old Charley fatally trapped in the ice, but this was the first time we had seen how quickly it could happen.

Grin finally tugged her right leg free but her left foot, so wide and awkward, was still caught beneath the surface. We used a pole to crack the ice and enlarge the hole she was caught in and though she was momentarily frightened, she was free. Now she was able to pick up the bread and the pool was useful to soften it in.

Gerry grabbed my hand. I thought she was slipping, but instead she was pointing to a pair of great black-backs who were flying in. Though much larger than our other gulls, they are so much lighter than the swans that they can stand on ice through which a Loh or Grin might fall and freeze. Powerful on land and in the air, they do not have to face most of the survival problems confronting the swans.

Two years ago there were none, last year we had that fatal pair, and now a second pair has moved in. And Gerry saw three more circling over the dunes yesterday. No matter how much the Gull Meister, Herr Tinbergen—with his impressive credentials—may admire them, for us here in the wetlands of eastern Long Island it means reinforcements from the north for the local war declared on swans and mallards and the other water-fowl pacifists.

143

And so, no longer the innocents of a year ago who believed our swans and cygnets would live happily ever after, we have come to another crucial April in the life cycle of Loh and Grin. They have gone back to the scene of the crime, to last year's nest, and they have rebuilt it into an imposing throne of reeds, three feet high, at least six feet long from stem to stern, and about five feet wide from one outside wall to the other.

We walked through the muck on the opposite bank, for a closer look. Grin was presiding from the top of this impressive construction, and Loh was stationed just outside the wall of reeds and mud that shielded it from the rising tide.

Today we saw Grin with her head down and her bottom up, high over her nest. Through the telescope we watched her struggle to push out a huge pastel egg that must have weighed a pound.

April is the month when we count the days until the cygnets hatch. But now that we have passed through one year of idyllic and triumphant rearing, and a second that turned out to be a laborious preparation for disaster, we are braced for what may come. Each day now, Loh and Grin take turns coming to the feed on our lawn. Waiting on the dock, dangerously close to their nest—like a pair of waterfowl muggers —are the giant gulls. There they sit, living death waiting to devour new life. What should we do?

Sometimes we talk of trapping these potential killers and sending them back to Canada where they belong. Sometimes, when we hear they are spreading south and multiplying, since the swans and other waterfowl are defenseless against them, we're tempted to take shotgun in hand and blast them out of the water. "Oh, but that would be interfering with nature!" cries a friend who goes by the book. To which we ask, "What about our own balance in nature? Are we not part of nature too? And since the Mute Swans have been better friends to man than man has been to them, isn't it time we interceded in their behalf to make up for the centuries of slaughter?"

We don't press our finger to the trigger. We buy decoys to frighten away the giant gulls. Gerry makes a precarious crawl out to the end of the rickety dock near the nest and attaches a plastic pinwheel that Refuge wardens recommend. It works—but only on the smaller gulls. When we report this failure back to the experts, they suggest owl decoys. We set up a pair of these formidable simulations near the nest, and it does seem to frighten the giant gulls away—for an hour. Then they return.

We look out at the nest of our brooding cob and pen and we wait for the clutch to hatch. We can only pray that the spirit of Lohengrin will suddenly materialize on our little inlet to champion Loh and Grin in their valiant effort to complete the cycle of mating, conception and birth so cruelly interrupted a year ago.

Here, on what we thought of as the serene, unthreatened Aspatuck, we seem to be living out our own version of *The Lady or the Tiger*. In the season of hope reborn, of the crocus, hyacinth and daffodil rising from their winter tombs, the season of Easter eggs, hatching swans, soaring expectations, is it to be

the cygnet or the predacious gull? The swan who kills nothing and acts out aggressive postures for self-protection, or the great black-back gull who kills everything he needs to survive and multiply?

Through Loh and Grin we have experienced all the myths and fairy tales, ballets, operas and human dramas that swans have inspired from the days of Apollo to this sweet but vulnerable season on the Aspatuck.

And so we wait...

Part V

I know of the sleepy country, where swans
*   fly round...*
A king and a queen are wandering there...
...so happy and hopeless, so deaf and so blind
With wisdom, they wander till all the years
*   have gone by...*

—W. B. Yeats

As the poet asked:
"...The last day shall we be very
Terrorized or merry?"